"AND LET THEM GATHER ALL THE FOOD OF THOSE GOOD
YEARS THAT COME, AND LAY UP CORN UNDER THE HAND OF
PHARAOH, AND LET THEM KEEP FOOD IN THE CITIES. AND THAT
FOOD SHALL BE FOR STORE TO THE LAND AGAINST THE SEVEN
YEARS OF FAMINE, WHICH SHALL BE IN THE LAND OF EGYPT;
THAT THE LAND PERISH NOT THROUGH THE FAMINE."

Genesis 41:35-36

A Quick Word

The intent of this seminar is to introduce the stark beginner to emergency preparedness by discussing the basic concepts we need to know in order to cover our bases in terms of the critical components for maintaining everyday life WITHOUT the infrastructure we normally depend on -- that is, without all our stuff.

We'll discuss the physical equipment and functions of daily life we need to focus our attention on and I'll dispel some popular myths. Hopefully you'll walk away with a clear roadmap for thinking about how YOU can start to be prepared for emergency conditions.

I must make a disclaimer before proceeding. We're talking about serious subjects here. Subjects which could mean the difference between life and death, hardship or comfort. We're talking about YOUR life, or the life of someone in your care. For this reason, please do not consider the information that follows to be concrete legal, medical, financial, or other advice. YOU are the only person who can decide the proper course of action for YOU. Everything I'm about to tell you is what I do, or MIGHT DO, in certain situations, based on my own personal experiences and research.

Gearing Up for Preparedness

As a young man I was heavily into scouting, took leadership roles, earned the Order of the Arrow and completed all of the coursework necessary for Eagle Scout. I continued to hike, hunt, fish, and train in various self defense schools. I'm a HAM radio operator, an FAA registered unmanned aeiral system pilot, and was certified as an NRA pistol instructor. At the age of fourteen I was paying close attention to domestic and international politics. I can accurately say that in one way or another, my life has incorporated reading the terrain and being prepared.

In 2013 I opened the Omega Outdoor & Emergency Supply Company in Dayton, Ohio. I operated this brick and mortar retail store, helping clients in our immediate area with advice, classes, and proper, high quality products for seven years. Recently, I closed that store and moved to a much more rural setting. I executed this large move of professional and private scope due to the deteriorating domestic conditions of 2019-2020.

When I speak to groups about preparedness, the attendees are usually already "sold" -- so to speak -- on at least one reason for being prepared. They, and perhaps you, already see and accept the need for emergency preparedness. It could be as simple as wanting to be prepared for a common winter power outage, or as doomy as being ready for a nationwide electromagnetic pulse, or "EMP", which shuts down the national power grid indefinitely.

As I am writing this presentation in early 2020, the Covid 19 scare has hit the world, driving home yet another reason why preparedness is a good idea.

Anything can happen at any time. A quick glimpse at history will verify that fact. It's just life.

I won't spend time describing the NUMEROUS scenarios which warrant us being prepared for emergencies, because that's an entire discussion in and of itself. As we regularly witness, we live in a world with no shortage of clear and present threats.

In October of 2008, the remnants of Hurricane Ike blew through Dayton. Tens of thousands were without power. Some for twenty days! Luckily for Daytonians, the weather was still warm and many people were only out of power for a few days -- but large enough swaths of people and stores *were* without power that supplies like bottled water were exhausted. People were driving almost 100 miles away to buy water. <u>Peoples' patience also started to become exhausted and some of the harder hit neighborhoods reported people getting a little squirrely, with light theivery and</u>

social temper tantrums springing up, confirming the theory that society has about 2-3 weeks of civility when essential services like electricity are removed.

When I talk about preparedness locally, I ask for a show of hands regarding who was out of power during that time. Routinely, 75% of the audience raises a hand.

My little informal poll always reminds me that it usually takes an "event" of some kind to smack us in the face before we become an active preparedness advocate and participant.

If *you* didn't need an event to wake yourself into a preparedness mindset, good for you! It is better to take advice, either your own or someone else's, than to pay the fool's tax of failure.

If it *was* an event that got you into preparedness, no matter -- **welcome aboard!** The preparedness community is glad to have you and I applaud the fact that you have recognized the threat(s) and are actively taking steps to mitigate your risk.

Every single prepared American means fewer people who need to rely on outside help. If you recall history, during WWII there were war bonds and patriot gardens. In my opinion, it's our patriotic duty as Americans to be able to fend for ourselves in times of crisis. This allows leaders to focus on the issues at hand *and* to reduce strain on local resources like grocery stores, police, fire, etc..

I also view it as a matter of national strategic importance; not only from a national defense standpoint, but also in regards to general national and local crisis management. Wouldn't a prepared America fare better?

Although you will find a "bitter prepper" from time to time, that is, a prepared person with an "I told you so attitude", I think you'll find most preparedness folks to be very willing, in fact, *eager* to share their expertise and thoughts in a helpful, non-condescending way.

They'll be happy that you're interested -- because most people aren't. If you honestly seek advice from a prepared friend, you are likely to become much, much better friends with that person. So if you know a "prepper", humbly reach out to him or her, explain what your concerns are and ask for some advice.

You should also be accessing books, videos, and information like this seminar.

A word of caution: On the internet you can find lots of good advice, but there's also very poor advice. Be wary of *any* advice you get. Do your own research when considering preparedness as you would any other course of study or hobby you might pursue in your professional or private life. Treat it as a serious endeavor.

Survival vs. Emergency Preparedness

The term "survival" calls up images of a bearded man with a crazed look in his eye cradling a tin of bourbon sitting in his bunker, rocking back and forth with a shotgun across his lap. . .waiting for the apocalypse.

While this type of person probably exists, I assure you that the vast majority of preparedness folks -- of the thousands I have met -- are NOT that person. YOU are not that person.

People with a preparedness mindset are respected tradespeople, realtors, lawyers, law enforcement, skilled craftsmen, fire and EMS, doctors, and more.

We are your next door neighbor. WE are you.

Don't let the negative stigma which has been associated with preparedness, largely due to "doomsday" television shows and scoffing media personalities, deter you from taking care of yourself.

Preparedness is no different than purchasing insurance. We purchase insurance for our vehicles, for our homes -- even for our lives. Why wouldn't we insure the food, water, supplies, and security for our daily needs?

If friends or family give you grief about your interest in preparedness, just smile and say, "Hasn't your power ever gone out?" Better yet, don't even bring up the subject. If you want to convince family and friends to get into preparedness for their own good (a noble cause), I've found that relating it to a local weather event is the best way to get them thinking positively.

A tornado, hurricane, winter storm, etc., are the best examples to get people to relate. If you lead off with an "apocalyptic scenario" like a meteor strike or EMP (ElectroMagnetic Pulse), no matter how real those threats are, you're likely not going to win any minds.

As we get into the meat of preparedness in the following pages, keep in mind that at Omega Outdoor, I focused on what is called "static home preparedness":

Static, meaning fixed in place, at home;

preparedness, which is what we do: Being ready for a change in normal daily life, having alternative ways to meet our daily needs.

Much of the equipment and products we utilize in preparedness have cross-over value in what some term "survival". The term "survival" is often conflated (related, or confused) with emergency preparedness.

My advice to you, specifically if you are just getting started in preparedness, is to focus on static home preparedness. "Survival" refers to living in the outdoors, away from home, with only what you can carry on your person -- and *there are very few people I know who have complete enough of a skill set to thrive in a true survival situation.*

After years and years of hearing people talk about the television show called "Alone", I finally binge-watched both available seasons. If you want to get a good idea of what it means to meet your day-to-day needs completely separated from society with no stores, no bikes, no motorcars, with minimal supplies, I urge you to watch that show. It will give you a good idea of what true outdoors survival means on a daily basis.

Even after studying preparedness and wilderness survival for years, I would struggle to meet my daily caloric requirement using only the "fat of the land".

I'm trying to do you a favor by dispelling the myth, which many in the preparedness community have delusions, of "going to the woods" to "live off the land".

It is not easy. You probably can't do it.

That's a hard pill to swallow for some, but I would be derilict in my duty if I didn't tell it to you straight.

If you or someone you know is operating under this line of thought, I strongly encourage that position be reconsidered. Test it. Do an experiment. Take your best guess at equipment and walk into the forest for a weekend with no food or water and see how things go. It will quickly become apparent whether you possess the skills to live with the land, or whether you need more training. On second thought, do NOT do that. Just imagine it honestly and you'll come to agree with me.

However, for those who have their heart set on being able to survive off the land, I recommend you start taking classes, reading books, and then actually going into the field to practice these skills. There are many respected and proven teachers of this skill set, which is often referred to as "bushcraft".

Emergency preparedness students should learn as many survival skills as possible, adding to your overall skill set and "survivability". The stark reality, though, is that few of us will become adept enough at these skills (or live in a region that is plentiful enough with wildlife and fauna) to thrive. Even fewer folks would actually *want* to live that lifestyle. It's hard, dirty work with few creature comforts.

<u>This presentation is about "static home preparedness".</u>

Once we've left our home we become refugees -- by definition -- and we don't want that.

The first option is stay at home, under shelter, with our all of our equipment.

"Bugging out" as some call it, in my opinion, is a last ditch option reserved for only the most serious of scenarios. Unless we have full-on societal breakdown, a "Mad Max" circumstance, I recommend going **nowhere.**

How and when to go somewhere is beyond the scope of this presentation.

Priority No.1: Clean Water

In studying survival techniques, you'll find that shelter is usually considered to be the number one priority. In static home preparedness, shelter -- *your house* -- is hopefully already an asset in place.

We'll come back to shelter later in this talk, but for now let's focus on what should be our number one priority for static home preparedness: <u>clean water</u>.

We all get a little "hangry" if we don't eat for six or eight hours, but dehydration is a much more dangerous condition than being hungry. Although not without discomfort and repercussions (like anger), the human body can live for weeks with little or no food.

Lack of water, though, will quickly lead to fatigue, confusion, headaches and a host of unpleasant conditions before the body shuts down completely and painfully.

Not the best state of mind when you need to make serious emergency-related decisions. With improper hydration, your mental and physical condition can deteriorate within hours and with no water at all, you'll be dead in several excrutiating days.

It's home preparedness 101: We need to secure a plentiful, renewable, and clean water source.

A good water-related experiment I ask clients to perform is to go to their favorite web-based mapping utility and use the "satellite" view to find their house, then slowly zoom out.

Not only does this "satellite view exercise" provide interesting tactical and intelligence data on your area, that is, good routes of travel, hideout spots, population density, home security ideas, etc., but as it relates to water, you may also find a stream, drainage ditch, retaining pond, or other suitable water source which you had no idea was so close at hand. With any luck, you will find this to be the case and if it is, you have good reason to take a fun hike and do some exploring. It might be a good time to strap on a back-pack you envision yourself carrying some supplies in and see how it goes with regards to your comfort.

If we want to be ready for emergencies, we can't rely on water coming out of the tap.

Even if water *is* coming out of the tap, we've likely all been under a boil advisory in the past. You can't count on the water from the tap in an emergency.

The best solution for securing clean water is a **water filter**. If water is plentiful in your area it's a no-brainer.

Having used water filters since I was a scout, I have to remind myself that many people are not even aware that personal water filters exist; and more importantly, that they WORK.

When you start researching water filters for purchase, you may find it confusing. There is talk about microns and percentages. There are many models available and while most will do the job, at least for a little while, some companies make outlandish claims with regards to the number of gallons their filter will clean and other filters are complicated to use.

Water filters fall into two general varieties:

> A. The kind that puts clean water directly into your mouth like a straw.
>
> B. The kind that will drip clean water into a container for later use.

The first, the direct to mouth filter, is usually a "straw" or bottle variety which, by sucking through a tube, you draw dirty water through the filter material directly into your mouth for drinking. The water that enters your mouth gets cleaned by that filter along the way, making it safe to drink.

I feel the best brand of straw type filter is a product called the "Lifestraw".

This company started with the sole intent of sending water filters to impoverished areas of the world which have poor water quality. They have a very good reputation and I trust them. I've seen people literally drink out of a toilet, from a manure and bug infested cow trough, and from scum laden ponds. . . *and none were sickened.* I'll take their word for it in these extreme filtration situations, but I have never been sickened using one with a "normal" woodland source like a creek.

While a straw type filter will keep you hydrated, my biggest concern with straw filters, and why I do not favor them ultimately, is because the clean water can only go one place: into your mouth.

What about water for coffee? For rehydrating food or cooking? For hygiene purposes like tooth brushing, hand washing, and washing dishes?

To accomplish these tasks, we need the second variety of water filter I mentioned.

It's the type of filter which will allow us to create potable water which can be collected and stored in clean water containers for use as needed.

My choice for home water filtration -- which is NOT reliant on electricity -- is the "Berkey" brand.

Berkey's **black** filter elements are expeditionary grade in quality and I personally trust them to make water safe to drink from ANY source. Puddles, ponds, etc..

The Berkey filtration unit features a two tank system made to sit on a kitchen countertop or other flat surface. In other words, it's not meant for backpacking. It's a table-top, home-based unit which varies in size from smaller than a breadbox to much bigger than a large microwave.

It's ingenious in its simplicity. Picture two buckets, one stacked on top of the other. The filtration elements are in the top bucket, which is where you pour the dirty water. Gravity causes the dirty water in the top tank to slowly be forced through the filters in that tank and as it does, it drips into the lower tank where the clean water gathers. The lower tank features a spigot for filling drinking cups and containers.

Three gallons of creek or pond water can be filtered in about six hours. Our family of five relies on a three gallon Berkey unit and we are never in need of water for our normal daily needs. We fill the upper tank from our kitchen faucet using a pitcher and we drink high quality water all day, knowing that it has been super-cleaned, while essential minerals are still present.

Here in the Midwest, we are blessed to have abundant water sources. I rest easy knowing that if we needed to, I could take large containers to a stream, river, or other nearby source, run the water through our Berkey system and have a nearly endless supply of potable water.

Just one set of black Berkey filters consistently lasts us nearly five YEARS -- and that's on iron rich well water.

If you have a pool, even better, because Berkey filters will remove the chlorine. You have 10-15,000 gallons of water just sitting in your backyard!

A Berkey is an expensive piece of equipment, ranging in price from $150 to $300, but keep in mind, that's the equivalent of nearly five years worth of clean water.

How much do you spend on bottled water in a year? More importantly perhaps, where would you even STORE five years worth of
water?

Water is heavy (at eight pounds per gallon) and it takes up a lot
of space. Most people don't have the room to store too much of
anything, let alone water. Just one more reason it's well worth the
front end investment.

I'll mention one more water filter you might consider.

This one is a portable filter, great for car kits, bags, hiking and
enjoyment, or even for daily use as a healthier water choice. It still
gives the advantage of letting you *create* and store potable water in
clean containers.

The name of this product is a "Grayl" water filter.

It looks like a water bottle and it works similarly to a coffee press.
You separate the inner shell from the outer shell, fill the outer
shell of the bottle with dirty water and then the inner shell is
pressed back into place. The filter is on the bottom of the inner
shell and as it is pressed into place, the dirty water is forced
through the filter, flowing into the clean inner bottle, ready for
drinking or for pouring into a clean container.

It's quite clever and I have come to really like these filters. At
$50 to $80 it's more affordable and, again, portable. Keep in mind
though, the filter capacity is much lower than that of a Berkey.
You'll top out around the 50 to 70 gallon mark per filter, but that's
enough water for one person for about two months. Replacement
filters cost around $20 each.

Berkey, the company that makes the table top units, also makes
a water bottle-type filter for use in the field. It utilizes the same
black element as in the table top version, only smaller. It's a little
easier to use than the Grayl, featuring a traditional-looking sili-
cone straw to sip. You fill the bottle, screw the lid back on and

squeeze the sport bottle as you drink from the straw. Very simple. This is usually the bottle I take with me into public because it looks more normal and it's easier to fill up and filter -- but again -- this type of filter only lets filtered water flow into your mouth. You can't create potable water to fill containers using this filter option.

I hope I've made clear the two general types of filters, the advantages and disadvantages of each:

One kind puts water only in your mouth, while the other allows you to fill containers -- keep this in mind when you are shopping for a water filter.

Whichever route fits your lifestyle and planning the best, I strongly urge you to find a water filtration method that will last. <u>Have extra filters on hand AND a back up filtering solution.</u>

Collecting water is also a useful idea.

If you own property, installing a rain barrel is a wise decision. There are many kits available at your local hardware store or online. Usually these kits involve cutting a small section from your downspout, inserting the water catchment section and then routing it to some sort of container. There are entire kits available, complete with a nice looking barrel, or you can home make as much of the unit as you like. Even the most novice handyperson can complete this project. There are many video tutorials online to view.

If you have your water filter, the water from your roof can be a valuable addition to not only your drinking and hygiene water security, but also to your garden plants' irrigation water security.

If a rain barrel is not in the cards for you, being ready with large tarps or even buckets to collect rainwater is something we can do in a pinch.

Also, consider filling up your bathtub if you know an impending storm is on the way which might cause a power outage. You can use your bathtub to store a large quanity of water indoors if need be, but again, a water filter is key to this plan if it's to be used for drinking.

Make sure your tub's stopper is water tight or you may lose all of your water to a slow leak.

Other emergency sources of water are your water heater, which can hold 30, 50, or even 100 gallons of already safe water; the back of the toilet, which takes water from a clean source; and there may be water still sitting in your garden hose.

Again, all of these sources are ones you would want to filter before using.

As with EVERY piece of equipment you purchase it's STRONGLY recommended that you use it. Familiarize yourself with it now while times are good to make sure it works. This way if you ever have to use it, you know what you are doing **and** exactly what need it will meet.

Now a few words about chemicals as an alternative way you can render drinkable (potable) water.

The benefits of chemical treatment are low, in my opinion, but they do have a place in preparedness. There are two benefits worth mentioning:

    A. Iodine tablets. A tried and true method of killing harmful protozoa. Two tablets will treat one quart (which is a standard size military canteen) in about 30 to 45 minutes, making it safe to drink from a biological standpoint.

    B. Chlorine dioxide, which i much prefer. One tablet will treat the same amount (1 quart), the downside being that it takes about 4 hours to work.

Chemicals are advantageous because they are small and light. Enough iodine or chlorine dioxide to last a month in the field can literally fit in the palm of your hand.

A major disadvantage to chemical water treatment is that it does nothing to *physically* remove sediment or other contaminants. You're not *removing* protozoa, you're just killing them, then drinking them. Same thing with dirt or mud. Kinda gross.

Don't get me wrong, chemicals will do the job and I *do* use chlorine dioxide and iodine from time to time, but it's not my cup of tea. Literally. *Taste* is another downside to chemical processing. Iodine tastes terrible. I regularly use flavored drink packets to make it more palatable. Frankly it's awful. As with anything, though, you can get used to it. An army ranger I know boasts that he uses iodine for a month at a time and it doesn't bother him at all. Yikes.

Chlorine dioxide on the other hand tastes more like pool water. It's drinkable with no further treatment and you won't make faces when it hits your palate. Still, it's not something you'd ask for at a restaurant. Keep in mind, as you'll read on the packaging for these chemicals, we're not supposed to consume them for much longer than a couple of weeks at a time.

You see now another reason why I prefer filters.

Chemical treatment is a great way to double up on making water safe if you think the water source is exceptionally dicey. Filter your water, then add chlorine dioxide tablets if you are really concerned about the water quality. You can also keep chemicals on hand when you're trying to make a kit as small as possible, or if you have a "quick emergency", but I would hesitate to rely on them as the ONLY way to get clean water. That's work for a full time water filter.

We should talk a bit about *storing* water.

A common line of questioning includes: "How long will water last?" and the closely related, "How do I make water store for a long time?"

My answer for both questions is: Water will "last" for millions of years. It just keeps going around and around the planet in different forms. Water is water is water.

The question people actually mean to ask is: "How can I store water and make it last so that I can drink it straight from the container?"

This is really what people want to know.

There is a product called "stabilized oxygen" and many people gravitate toward it as a solution for this issue. It's a bit expensive, but it can be added to clean water in a clean container to keep biological growth from occurring during long term storage. I have used it in the past and it appeared to work.

BUT, as I stared at my *very clean-looking* five YEARS old water barrel, I found myself hesitant to just stick a straw in and drink straight from the barrel.

The water *looked and smelled clean*, but I couldn't bring myself to drink straight from the barrel. So I ran the water through my water filter and everything was fine. Now we're back to where we started. Filtration.

Experience taught me that my idea of water storage was flawed. Our preparedness mindset will evolve over time, or it *should* evolve, as we learn and experiment.

Always do what works for YOU.

Instead of focusing on how to *keep* water potable, I should have realized I'd want to clean the water again just to be sure. My current practice is to make sure the container I'm using is clean (by swishing a chlorine based water solution around inside it, then air drying). I then add the requisite number of drops of Chlorox, <u>unscented</u> bleach, based on water volume. It's a very small amount of bleach and I will let you do your own research as to how much to use per gallon. This should keep biologicals from growing in your water. Remember, even if things do grow in your water, we're going to filter the water anyway.

Store your water, like most everything else we want to preserve, <u>in a cool, DRY, and dark place</u>, keeping light from entering the water container. (This also goes for rain barrels if possible -- they should be opaque at the least.) Then be prepared to filter the water upon use.

In this way, there is no need to try and *keep* the water drinkable straight from the container.

I assure you that after 5 years, you are going to end up filtering it anyway simply for the mental peace of mind.

A few final thoughts on water...

If you have to procure water in the field, try to find the clearest-looking water you can. A moving stream is best, scooping water from the very top of the stream as close to the center of the stream as possible. The deeper and faster flowing, the better.

If you MUST use dirty or turbid water containing lots of sediment, try as best you can to pre-filter that water before running it through your actual water filter. *The cleaner the water, the longer your filter will last.*

Stretch an old t-shirt or towel over a five gallon bucket (or other container) and pour heavily dirtied water through it. You can set up a series of buckets, moving your water on down the line until it gets as clear as possible using crude fabric filtration, *then* utilize your desired method of making water drinkable: A filter, chemicals, or even boiling it.

By the way, boiling water (which is often advised as a "boil advisory") is the last method you want to count on for clean water. It's time consuming, fuel consuming, you have to wait for it to cool to use -- generally just a large pain in the rear to execute. What if the power is out and you have an electric stove? Even if you have a propane grill, you'll burn tons of propane boiling water which you may need for cooking food.

I hope this section has provided a basic understanding and direction for further research on water procurement, cleaning, and storage.

Mama Can't Be Hangry: Storage Food

Representing another evolution in my preparedness thinking, I've moved to advising my clients that up to 80% of their preparedness income should be spent on shelf stable foods, otherwise known as "storage food".

80%!

There are tons of neat gadgets and preparedness supplies to distract us, but the vast majority of our funds should be spent on securing as much food as possible.

Most storage food companies tout a twenty-five year PLUS shelf life when stored properly; that is, stored in a cool, DRY, and dark location -- not in the attic. This is an investment in the future, not something you'll need to replace every few years like a pair of boots.

In speaking with a major manufacturer (who will remain nameless), "off the record" I've been told that they have sampled FIFTY year old products and it tasted perfectly fine. When you remove water and oxygen from food (or anything), it lasts a very, very long time.

Take note that we rarely hear about people getting dehydrated in Venezuela or other places with problems.

We DO hear about starvation and fights over food.

Look back to history, think about how food has been used as a weapon against populations for thousands of years. So has water. Water is much easier to find and process than is our full caloric needs for each day.

Think about it. Even if you're boiling water to make it safe for use, so long as you can find water, this is a half day process. Growing potatoes, or even lettuce, takes weeks and/or months, plus proper growing conditions. Food, friends, is THE most important commodity to have in your possession at this point.

I spoke about being "hangry" earlier and how it's not as immediate a problem as is dehydration. That said, let's face it -- being hangry *is* a problem.

My delicate flower of a wife gets "hangry". (I've hereby been instructed to note that my wife should be referred to as a "delicate flower" but that she's really a warrior.)

On vacations or just at home, if mama bear gets hungry, we need to fix that problem immediately. I'm half joking, but *this speaks to food first becoming a MORALE issue.*

When we are fed, we are happy. When we are hungry, we tend to get testy -- and that can lead to poor decision making and general strife. You've probably witnessed this phenomena yourself under normal everyday circumstances just waiting in line at a restaurant.

Ultimately, and more importantly than morale, *food is required to keep us alive.* We need it for more reasons than to keep mama happy. It's an obvious point, but I can't tell you how many times I've seen clients waste money on items in our store when they have not yet secured their food supply (despite my best efforts to steer them properly).

At the time of this writing in June of 2020, tired as I am with having to talk about Covid 19, the current situation has driven home the point of preparedness.

Here in Ohio, the meat and canned goods sections of the grocery store look alarmingly sparse at times. At this point, I still can't find yeast for bread making. The other day, there was no corn starch. Many sources and news outlets are talking about meat shortages in the not too distant future, as many of our ranchers are being put out of business by regulation.

How would our currently highly divided social structure/society react if America started looking like Venezuela? What if food became a scarce commodity?

I have personally witnessed small scale riots when electronic benefit cards (EBT) (the modern equivalent of food stamps) stopped working at the local grocery store. This is when times are *normal* and food is *plenty*. It's not hard to imagine what an actual food shortage would look like and how people would react.

If I had my wish, every single American would have a MINIMUM of 6 months of storage food on hand.

It's also worth mentioning that, having been in preparedness for over 20 years, the price of food, *specifically meats* has, and continues to, go through the roof.

A large "Number 10" can of dehydrated chicken cubes used to cost $25. It's now over $50.oo per can! 30% of that rise in cost happened in the past two years (2018-2020). We don't get that kind of return on our money when we put it in a bank, so perhaps we should re-consider where we put our money.

Furthermore, who is to say that chicken will even be *available* to purchase two years from now?

They're trying to move us to eating cricket burgers. Go look that up. There is a concerted effort by certain factions to move society away from meat products all together. Bill Gates, to drop one name, has invested heavily in a non-meat "burger" product. Will we even be "allowed" to eat meat in 20 years if certain factions have their way? Cows emit too much methane, right? There is a movement to do away with cow farming. It sounds like science fiction, but a bit of research will reveal the truth. Couple this with another research topic you may want to explore (the Grand Solar Minimum) and you'll quickly realize the importance of food security.

With a twenty-five (25) year-*plus* shelf life, the can of chicken that costs $50.oo today, could easily cost over $100.oo per can in the near future. That is an investment I am very willing to make: Freezing my food cost for twenty-five years at today's prices.

Keep in mind, you can't eat money, gold, or bullets.

Similar to a high-quality water filter, the front end price tag of a six (6) month supply of food looks high (and it is), but the store of value and security it provides is well worth the strain on our wallets. Once you have a food supply, you have it. In hand. It becomes priceless.

A wise man once told me: If you don't hold it in your hand, you don't own it.

Get your food supply and you can check that box off your list of must-haves.

When selecting storage food, there are several routes you can take and there's no lack of different manufacturers these days, each with their own sales pitch, advantages and disadvantages. There are a few companies which stand out for various reasons, but before I mention specific brands, let's talk about a couple more aspects of food storage.

Choose to store the things you like to eat.

If you're gluten intolerant, it would be wise to store fruits, vegetables, and meats rather than beef stroganoff with pasta. If you like spaghetti, store spaghetti. If you like broccoli, store broccoli. Almost any food is available commercially, or is able to be self-stored at home. There is no need, nor sense, in storing or purchasing rice if you hate rice. (Perhaps for trading.)

You can create your own meal plan, or you can go for the buckets of pre-selected meal combinations.

It might be more work at first to create your own meal plan, rather than buying a shotgun approach six month, pre-determined food supply, but in the end you will be happier if you store what you like to eat.

For most of us, we're not picky eaters and the pre-selected meal packages will work just fine.

Another school of thought says that if you're starving, you'll eat ANYTHING -- and like it. The smart money says that idea is most likely true. Even the worst boxed meal would taste like mama's home cookin' if it was the only thing you'd had to eat in 48 hours.

What is storage food anyway?

Many new clients we saw at Omega Outdoor had a bad taste in

their mouths for this mysterious "storage food" even though they had never tried any.

Storage food, though, I assure you, is prepared in the same way as the boxed meals we find in the grocery store. Pre-cooked food is either freeze dried or dehydrated, then packaged, usually in a box, sometimes in a pouch. Think macaroni and cheese.

Sometimes flavoring packets or certain ingredients are in separate envelopes in the box, sometimes not. It's a pretty common industry practice and if you go look at a box meal in your cupboard right now, you'll find that the expiration date is about two years.

The difference?

Packaging -- it's the only difference.

If you were to put the contents of a box meal in your cupboard into an appropriate container, such as a *mylar bag*, and add an *oxygen absorber*, you would have twenty-five year shelf life food, packaged as it would be by a storage food company!

You can do this at home.

You can pack already dried foods yourself, if you want to take the time and make the effort. For our more experienced clients, we carried numerous different sizes of mylar bags and oxygen absorber packets for self-packing foods at home.

If you are unfamiliar with "mylar", it's the metalicized material from which the shiny party balloons are made. You're no doubt familiar with those types of balloons that stay on the ceiling for months at a time, long after the party has ended, while the less expensive latex rubber balloons are on the floor the very next day.

The reason for this is that the mylar material allows for a very low rate of gas exchange. Just like helium gas, oxygen and moisture also have a very hard time penetrating the mylar material. Food storage bags are made of this same material. Mylar balloons are generally very thin, while the mylar used for food storage is thicker, making it even less permeable. Oxygen is the enemy of food storage and mylar is one of the solutions.

If you'd like to try your hand at packing your own food, you can find supplies from numerous sources. A great source on the web is Sorbent Systems. Just search for "sorbent systems mylar" and I'm sure you'll find them. They have a wide variety of mylar bags and oxygen absorbers at reasonable prices.

Mylar bags can be heat sealed with a normal clothes iron at home and you can find numerous videos on Youtube showing you how to do this. It's easy.

Once you have your dehydrated or freeze dried food of choice sealed in mylar with an appropriately sized oxygen absorber, the only thing left to do is to put your freshly self-packed bag of storage food into a *vermin proof* container. Mylar is great for oxygen and moisture protection, but the gnawing teeth of mice and animals can decimate your food storage, so we must also guard against that.

When you look at pre-made food supplies, you'll notice most all come in some sort of plastic bucket or container. The bucket is not meant to keep the food fresh. Vermin are the reason for this (as well as for convenience in storage and moving). So by all means, try your hand at some self-prepared food storage as it can save you well over 50% in costs and open up more variety; but be sure to prepare and protect it properly.

Remember, again, once you have secured food, you want to put it in a *cool, DRY, and dark place.*

We don't want to have wasted all that time, money, and effort in storing food, only to have a mouse ruin it or worse, have it mold and mildew or otherwise prematurely age by having put it in the attic (which is prone to massive temperature swings throughout the year).

A big convenience of pre-packaged storage food is the way we prepare it for consumption.

Dehydrated food only requires that you add boiling water, stir, allow it to sit for 10 to 15 minutes, stir it again and you're ready to eat. Very simple.

Freeze dried food is a little different, more like a simmer meal, in which we stir it over heat for 15 to 20 minutes. It's a little more labor intensive, but the trade off is usually the level of quality. Freeze dried food, in my opinion, is a little tastier. The trade off for dehydrated is convenience when it comes to preparation.

While we're on the topic of *preparation*, think about *how* you're going to prepare food, even if it's just boiling water. If you have an electric range top and the power goes out, it's not going to work. A great item to make an excuse to purchase, if you don't already have one, is a propane grill.

We do a lot of grilling around here even in the winter and you can cook for a long time on a couple of tanks of propane. My favorite preparedness items are those which I get to use on a regular basis, like our grill. We get our money's worth from the investment that way and you get to know your equipment inside and out.

If you have no interest in a full size grill, there are many small camp stoves available (a discussion of which exceeds the scope of this presentation). Some of these stoves are small enough to fit in the palm of your hand, others are table top units, all using a variety of fuels and ranging in cost from around $30 to in excess of $150.

Stoves like these give you the ability to cook at home or in the field. The traditional and ubiquitous Coleman style camp stove which takes the small, green bottles of propane are something we've probably all seen at some point in life as they are widely available in any big box store and are very popular with campers. They are usually green or red in color, open like a clam shell and have wind shields on three sides. they're very easy to use, not too large, and the fuel is readily available.

Back to pre-packed storage food.   With regards to the different brands, I'll mention a few here in general commentary. Each company has a different way of presenting their sales pitch, but the rubber hits the road at *price per calorie* and quality.

You'll see a lot of sales pitches according to the number "servings". 60 servings of this, 120 servings of that.

Well, just how much IS a "serving"? How many calories are in that "serving"? _Calories are the name of the game_.

I have seen one company that markets a "1 month" food supply and while the dollar value wasn't bad calorie-wise -- the total number of calories for their so-called 1 month supply was less than 20,000.

To maintain daily caloric need for one person, for 30 days' nutrition, I put the number of calories the average person needs (per month) at about 45,000 -- more than *double* what the supposed 1 month food supply provided. How many people purchased that kit and assumed it had enough food for 1 month?

While you could *live* on 20,000 calories a month, you'd hardly be well-fed and I'm sure you'd be unhappy with your purchase.

Again, what we want to calculate is **number of calories versus cost**. Some companies make this easy and some seem to try and deliberately hide it.

You need to determine how many calories YOU need for one month. This will vary from person to person based on age, activity level, and perogative. I cannot determine this for you. You'll also want to calculate the cost of the food *in calories*.

Legacy Food Storage does a great job of showing you all of this information up front: How many pounds of food is in a particular package deal, the total number of calories, the amount of cubic space the package takes up (which is nice), and of course, the price. Legacy is also one of the most economical choices.

Wise Storage Food brand is economically similar to Legacy, although they don't make it as easy to ascertain how many calories per dollar you're getting. From a quality standpoint I find these two companies to be on pretty level playing ground, advantage Legacy, due to more up front marketing practices.

Another common question I get is: "Which storage food is best?"

When it comes to taste, personally (and tastebuds differ), I have to split the award between My Patriot Supply and Mountain House.

Mountain House, also known as Oregon Freeze Dried, is the oldest storage food company around, having contracted with the US Military for decades. They also largely cater to backpackers with trail-ready meals. Their menu is well-defined and locked into place, rarely adding new additions. When they do add a new item, it's usually quite good, holding up to the standard they have set. Chicken and dumplings and biscuits and gravy, for example, are two newer meals and they are both great. They've been in the game a long time.

Praise for Mountain House aside, their meals also have a high sodium content. Also, they only offer their meals in the large steel number 10 cans, or in the smaller, more expensive trail-ready pouches which do not feature the same varieties.

Number 10 cans are great for storage purposes. You can't beat a number 10 can. It's durable, vermin proof, and air tight. Mountain House has vegetables, fruits, meats, and pre-mixed meals like chicken teriaki and beef stroganoff. You will end up developing your own food plan from these choices if you go with Mountain House, so it's a little more work for the beginner, but the individual number 10 can approach can be very helpful. It lets you round out a meal plan with specific items like green beans, corn, apples, or a meat, rather than having to take what is predetermined in a package deal.

My Patriot Supply touts a non GMO menu, if that is attractive to you, and a lower sodium content (although not by much). You'll also pay more. Their meals are the freeze dried "simmer" variety, which requires a bit more work on the front end to prepare the meals, while Mountain House and Wise allow you to simply add boiling water, stir and wait for the food to rehydrate.

For being a newer company, My Patriot Supply has done well to create very good tasting meals. Most of their packages, like those of Wise and Legacy, are predetermined, as opposed to Mountain House, again, which has individual number 10 cans of a variety of items.

You'll also find other canneries like Grandma's Country Foods, Nutristore and Auguson Farms (usually based out of Utah) which have oddities and base level ingredients like sugar, baking powder, butter powder, powdered peanut butter, salt, and even popcorn -- all sealed nicely in number 10 cans.

I have found that no ONE food company can meet all of my needs. I end up going to six or seven different companies to fill out the larder with the what I want.

Remember, you can always pack your own food in order to get *exactly* what you want -- usually at a better price. It all comes down to what you will **do**.

*We need to get the job done and secure our food supply.

If you know in your heart that packing your own food is too much of a hassle and you're going to procrastinate, then just pay the money for pre-packed and be done with it. Whatever you decide to do after having heard the basics we are discussing now (water and food) -- do NOT put if off any longer. Get it secured.

Immediately.

The type of food we've been discussing is for storage. It's the last resort food that you don't want to dip into unless there's a real food emergency.

Your first line of defense for food security should be your normal, everyday pantry.

Grandmas and depression era family members (if you're lucky

enough to still have any around) would tell you that our best investment in life is a well stocked pantry. I'm sure I'm not the only one who's heard that wisdom. Canned and dried goods you have on hand right now, today, in house, should be able to last your household at least 1 month without having to go to the store for ANYTHING. This is the bare minimum.

Don't make the rookie mistake, which I have heard at Omega Outdoor numerous times over the years, of having a "bunch of canned goods in the basement" for emergencies. I'm here to tell you that 5 years goes by quickly and those canned goods are going to be expired before you know it. If the time comes that you need them, you're not going to *want* to eat them simply from a psychological standpoint.

You need to purchase new goods, eat the older ones in the cupboard first, and continue to rotate your stock as you cook normally. In this way, you end up with ZERO old canned goods and everyone is happy. Simply buying a couple of extra cans per trip to the store can easily fill out a pantry in a month or two's time without breaking the budget. Everyone can do this. Once your initial stock is in place, there is no need to buy extra when shopping. Just purchase the normal number of cans when you shop once your extra supply is set.

Now let me expound on, and adjust, my comments regarding "old" canned goods:

I'll tell you about the *myth* of expiration dates.

Obviously you should use your own judgement, but if the can is not cracked or leaking, if it's not bulging, if it hasn't been stored improperly -- odds are that the food will be good for long, long past the expiration date.

In fact, 100 year old and older canned goods are unearthed from time to time from places like the antarctic or deep in the mud of the mississippi river. Usually, they're still perfectly safe to eat! Scientists routinely run such foods through tests and find them to be free of harmful bacteria, having only lost single digit percentage values of their vitamin content. 100 years, safe to eat, and almost 90% of their nutritional value preserved! That's pretty amazing.

The other test you can and *should* utilize is a good old fashioned smell test. There have been numerous academic studies regarding this as well. Blind studies show that humans can tell with 95% accuracy whether food is bad or good just by smelling it. So your mom was right, there's nothing wrong with that tuna salad in the fridge. Check the can for damage or signs of bulging, then open and smell.

The reason I say you won't *want* to eat canned goods past the expiration date is because the *look* of the food won't be as appetizing and the *texture* when eating it will change -- neither for the better. There's also the psychological aspect. We just don't like eating food that says "it's expired".

For these reasons, it's best to just rotate and eat canned goods as though they DO expire. It's more of a morale issue than one of safety.

Depending on how deeply you want to get into preparedness, perhaps an expanded every day pantry with boxed and canned goods, rotated properly, will meet your needs for a month or two of food security. That may be as far as you want to get into preparedness.

If, on the other hand, you want to be prepared for longer than a month or two, I recommend looking into the long-term shelf life foods, either the pre-prepared or self-packed types previously described.

No matter which direction you decide to go for food, keep these key pieces of advice in mind: Calculate your caloric needs and store what you like to eat.

...but most importantly of all, just get it done!

Will Your Cave Weather the Storm?

Shelter is an important aspect of survival, but we tend to think of it less when it comes to static home preparedness. Why? Probably because we (hopefully) already have a roof over our heads.

What IS shelter anyways? What does it mean to us?

Shelter provides many things. Protection from the elements, of course: rain, wind, cold and sun; but it also provides a place to complete tasks like cooking, sleeping, and conducting hygiene.

What follows are a few things to think about when it comes to the shelter we call our HOME.

I said that Dayton was lucky when Hurricane Ike's remnants blew through. We were lucky that it was *warm* weather and not the dead of winter. A two week power outage in sub-freezing temperatures can quickly turn into a disaster. People can live in cold conditions, but if you can't heat your home, water pipes are in danger of freezing and rupturing.

The only thing worse than no power for two weeks in the winter is no power for two weeks in the winter with a swimming pool in your basement *and* no water from the faucet, no hot water, no heat.

You need to either know how to drain your entire water system in the case of such an eventuality, or you have to be able to supply off grid heat to keep the pipes from freezing all together.

The first idea is simple enough to learn how to do, albeit a bit of a hassle. The second option is much better because it affords us to continue to live in a fairly normal fashion. We can still use the toilet and get water from the faucet, even if it's a bit colder than usual in the house without normal heating.

When it comes to off grid heat for a normal house, there is but one solution: Fossil fuels.

My favorite method is a wood burning Buck Stove. It has an electric blower (which I'll get back to in a minute). A good wood stove can provide more BTUs (heat) than conventional HVAC systems and usually fuel wood is plentiful, depending on your location.

Other options include propane powered units like Mr. Heeter, as well as kerosene heaters which, although less common these days are still available at local hardware stores. If used properly, both of these options are safe and relatively inexpensive. They can be placed strategically to provide just enough heat to make things your home function and stay liveable.

Whole house generators are another way to go to try and keep your home operable when the electric goes out, but keep in mind if you are on electric heat you would need a very high output, more expensive generator. Even then, a generator will only supply modest supplemental electric heat, likely not to exceed 60 degrees, which is less than ideal.

If natural gas or fuel oil is your heat source, it won't be a problem for a smaller whole house generator as only the electric blower needs to run on electricity (as opposed to furnaces with electric heating elements).

Most generators are going to consume around 1.5 gallons of fuel per hour, regardless of which fuel type it uses. A five-hundred gallon propane tank for a whole-house generator sounds like a lot, but it won't last quite as long as you might think it would -- only about a week! For short term preparedness, which is what we're going to experience most often in the form of a winter storm, etc., a whole house generator can provide the creature comforts like hot water and refridgeration to keep people happy. Remember though, they have a high rate of fuel consumption and for this reason we can't rely on them for long term preparedness.

The system I have set up in our house features a small, 5000 watt generator on wheels and a separate electrical panel which feeds just FOUR essential services to the house: Our well pump (for water), the Buckstove outlet (for blowing the stove's heat), a chest freezer, and the refridgerator. With these four features, we'll continue to have water... heat, which is also a way to cook... and our spoilable food stays preserved. All essential services remain in tact, although no hot showers.

The downside to electrical power reliance and generation using fossil fuels is that eventually you will run out of natural gas, propane, or fuel.

This is where solar comes in.

I keep a large battery on hand which is charged with a 150 watt solar panel. Between the battery and intermittant running of the gas generator, it's enough to keep this battery fully charged so we can run the air blower on the woodstove. We don't need to run our generator full time. We can run it for a few hours every four or five hours to keep the coolers cool, the woodstove running, the water in stock, and the batteries charged. Operating our generator in this way expands our fuel supply window by 2 or 3 times and reduces maintenence requirements on the generator.

Getting into solar can be expensive and confusing. It's another topic that is too complex for this introductory presentation. At the very least, check out a product line called "Goal Zero". You can purchase a good quality solar panel (and batteries) for charging phones, laptops and more, all using solar power. Their products are "plug and play" in nature, very simple to use and give you a strong leg up in a power down situation. It's a good way to dip your toe into solar power and start learning what it can do for you. It is expensive, though.

Hopefully you're starting to see how the "shelter" we call our homes may not be so impervious to problems.

Next, let's talk about the duty no one wants to talk about: doo dee.

If your pipes freeze, or if you drain your system of water, how will you flush the toilet?

You can bring in water from the outside to fill the back of your toilet tank to get it to flush, but can you get unfrozen water? In the summer this is not a problem. If you can find water, you can flush your toilet even if you don't have power or water pressure.

So flushing indoor plumbing may, or may not be a problem, but consider this: If you're on a city sewage system, rather than a self contained septic system found in more rural settings, the city system can back up as a result of power outages or even high precipiation events -- *right into your basement.*

As with frozen/burst pipes, this situation would render your house uninhabitable.

The only way you could avoid that nightmare would be to install a main drain shut off valve (which may not be allowed under zoning codes). If one did install such a shut off valve it might save your basement, but keep in mind there is also no *outflow* possible, so you also can't flush *your* toilet. You'd have to figure out another way to dispose of waste.

All of these problems are able to be solved, as usual.

Turning off the water to your toilet and draining the bowl by flushing it will allow you to put a heavy ply trashbag under the toilet seat. A small can of fine, dry dirt, or sawdust kept near the commode lets you grab a scoop and dust over each use to keep odors down.

Urination is done in a separate container and could be easily disposed of in a prepared, gravelled trench outside. The details of these methods are something we should be thinking about and researching in case we need to employ them.

Related to waste disposal is water.

We've touched on water filtration and procurement, but think about it in terms of how water relates to your current shelter. We are used to turning the spigot and instantly having clean water, but if you are on a well and the power goes out there will be no water. Likewise, if you're relying on the city for water, it's either provided via electric pumping stations or, more likely, via a gravity water tower (which also requires electric pumping to fill the resevoir).

Water *towers* are better for us in an emergency because they are kept full and will deliver water pressure until empty. They will, however, empty quickly -- perhaps in as little as 24 hours. Some municipalities have back up generators to deal with power outages, but are generally only prepared for 3-7 days contingency. Once past this period, all bets are off.

In the case of both water and sewage, when relying on city services it's best to not count on more than two weeks of coverage.

Think about what you would do, what would happen, if we moved into a 30 to 60 day period.

Would you still *have* "shelter"?

Or would you be forced to abandon your home due to one or more of the problems discussed?

All of this doesn't even broach the physical security aspect of sheltering in place during a calamity. I will talk a little about security in the next section.

Medical Supplies & Security

There are week long and longer courses which focus *soley* on medical supplies and training. As you know, doctors go to school for quite some time, but we can all approach the level of EMT/EMS training.

Each of the topics we've discussed so far could be expounded upon almost ad infinitum, but medical is one of the more complex.

I recommend having at least a standard, over the counter medical kit. It should be in the $30-$50 range. For this type of kit, I like the ones which come in a hard plastic case with several layers to it.

Starting with such a kit -- one manufactured by Johnson & Johnson for example -- will provide a variety of items like burn cream, anti-itch wipes, antiseptics, antibiotics, larger gauze pads, bandaids, and possibly some less common over the counter medications like allergy pills, anti-diarreahals and medication for constipation. As usual, the more you pay, the better the kit will be.

When you get your kit home, immediately go through each and every pocket or separator. For home use kits, I prefer the plastic box type variety with separated containers because they're easier to keep organized. Go through each and every item and take the time to learn what it is and what it and what it does. Use the internet to learn about each item, or better yet, invite a medically familiar friend over to discuss the kit. Then, reassemble the kit in a way that makes sense to YOU.

In taking these steps, you'll become knowledgeable about exactly *where* things are in the kit for quick access in an emergency, and exactly *what* you can treat.

Once you have this relatively simple kit...

    A. You will have quickly taken care of most common and immediate medical needs that can be treated at home.

    B. You will have a good starting point to expand your knowledge and supply of medical equipment into the future.

Depending on the style of container your kit comes in, there may be extra room which will allow you to build a more comprehensive kit by adding items.

I do not encourage you to purchase a medical kit in excess of $100 as your first step into medical supplies. If you don't know how to use a blood pressue cuff or nasopharyngial airway, there's really no need for you to have it at this point. Some people will argue that they might "come across a doctor" who knows how to use things in a complex kit, but in all liklihood it will either never be needed or you will *not* "come across" someone. I recommend saving the money until you can learn how to use more complex medical supplies yourself OR you know for a fact there will be a medical professional in your preparedness circle.

While a standard over the counter medical kit has the advantage of being a wide shotgun spread of useful items and it's a *great* teaching tool, the drawback of these kits is that you'll only get one or two of any particular item. This means the first time you have to address a burn is likely the last time you'll be able to address a burn unless you purchase more burn cream.

This is why over the counter kits are great TEACHING tools and very useful, but as your knowledge expands you will quickly realize your journey has just begun.

See what's in the kit, then expand it by purchasing more of what is in it, usually at cheaper prices. Some things you probably won't need too many of, like anti itch wipes. Others, such as good-quality *cloth* bandaids and antibiotic ointments you will want to have *hundreds* of and here is an anecdote to drive that home:

On family vacation, my daughter, in bare feet after swimming, opened a door which scraped right over her big toe, peeling back a layer of skin. It made a pretty good little injury. It was painful and exposed to infection. We were prepared with our medical kit. SIXTEEN bandaids and two packets of antibiotic ointment later, the wound was healed without further incidence, praise God.

The point is, you will likely go through commonly used items quicker than you may think. Specifically, bandaids and antibiotic ointment. The most *common* injuries will be small, yet requiring attention to prevent infection, serious outcome, and to promote healing.

Giant gauze pads for catastrophic injuries, hopefully, will never even have to be used, so it is prudent to have less of those. Common bandaids, though, buy boxes.

If there are any medications routinely taken by you or family members, that is something you want to try to stock up on. If genuine and responsible concern is stressed with your family doctor, they may write you a prescription to stock up a few months' supply. If not, it will be on *you* to figure out what to do about stockpiling.

As usual, thinking ahead is crucial.

A critical item I recommend adding to over-the-counter-grade medical kits is a CAT tourniquet, which stands for **Combat Application Tourniquet**.

A tourniquet is used to stop severe bleeding, usually of an arterial nature. These wounds typically squirt or ooze blood in hearty volumes and in such a case only a tourniquet will save a life by stopping all bloodflow.

You can make a tourniquet the old fashioned using a belt, a piece of clothing or rope, but it's much quicker, easier, and less stressful to have this $30 item on hand ready to go. Watch out for fakes. Real CATs are made by a company called North American Rescue and you WILL pay $30 for one. The fakes are almost indiscernable from the genuine article, but are usually priced in the $15 to $20 range. <u>Get the real thing</u>. The fakes are known to break during use -- a terrible time to have skimped on a product.

One more item to consider adding for catastrophic injury is something called an "Israeli bandage". This is a combat dressing available to the public, which is essentially a large gauze pad pre-attached to an Ace-style elastic bandage. It comes in bombproof packaging and is easily applied to a wide variety of serious injuries. It can even be used as a rudimentary tourniquet. Price range on Israeli bandages is anywhere from $10-$20, depending on the size. I recommend having at least a 4" and a 6" Israeli bandage with your kit. These two items -- the battle dressing and the CAT tourniquet -- will allow you to treat life threatening injuries.

Medical supply is a huge rabbit hole. I highly recommend you embark on a course of self study or better yet, find a local class. Think about auditing a college level course for EMT students. You needn't pass the course, but you *will* get all of the knowledge that comes with that level of training -- and that's invaluable.

A couple of books I will mention are "When There Is No Doctor" and "When There Is No Dentist". These books were written as field manuals for missionaries who go to remote villages in countries with little infrastructure. The subject matter of these books delves into the next level of preparedness. They are so valueable, I felt they should be mentioned.

Take the Covid 19 virus of 2020 again as an example. People could not get masks for love or money in the early days of the fiasco. Guess what is in most medical kits: gloves, masks, hand sanitizer and more. Yet another homage to being prepared.

Many people tried to avoid going to the hospital during Covid 19 for fear of getting infected. It's a valid line of thought. In a pandemic circumstance, the hospital really IS the last place we want to go if at all possible. That's where the sick people go. The ability to treat wounds and conditions at home provides a nice advantage no matter the circumstances. Just another reason medical supplies and training are important when we are getting into a preparedness mindset.

The final topic for your entry level seminar is one I have prioritized both as our #1 concern, as well as possibly in the #5 position. I still bounce around on the philosophy of the order of prioritization myself.

The topic is self defense.

The reasoning behind self defense being #1 on our list of priorities -- even above water -- is the idea that if we can't *protect* something. . .do we really HAVE it?

If someone can *take* your water, do you really even have the water at all?

It's an interesting concept, but then again, if you don't have water in the first place, you *also* don't have it. You can see how it's a bit of a quandry. Chicken or the egg?

Regardless of where you decide to fall in that philosophy, the bottom line is that self defense makes the top 5 priorities list, so it's still important.

When the topic is self defense, people often think of *firearms*. I am an advocate of firearms, being a fan of our great Constitution. I know it was put there because it's our God-given right as individual free people to protect ourselves from those who would do us harm by any means available. That said, and as a former NRA instructor, firearms are NOT for everyone.

By that, I mean each individual should *explore* the world of firearms through study, *training,* through speaking with others, and most importantly with *thorough introspection* and thought in order to determine whether or not he or she should even own a firearm.

If you are not 100% certain you can decisively fire on a criminal who is trying to do harm to you or others, do not buy or carry a gun.

Lives are lost when a gun owner has their own firearm taken from them and used by the criminal. I have advised several clients and friends to NOT purchase a firearm after having spoken with them extensively.

If your personality and convictions *are* compatible with firearms ownership, more power to you! If not, it will be safer to go another route. Firearms ownership is not to be taken lightly and we should give it the proper respect and forethought.

My solution, should a firearm not be in your future?

Pepper spray.

Even though I carry a firearm daily, I also carry pepper spray. I do this for several reasons. *First, I don't want to shoot anyone.* If all I have are my fists, feet, and a pistol, I will be forced to use one of those options. When I add pepper spray to my toolbox, I add a level of force which is outside of physical confrontation *and* deadly force.

When you draw a firearm, or even strike someone, it changes the dynamic of the confrontation both physically, as well as legally in the eyes of the justice system. YOU may be inappropriately raising the level of force in the confrontation, which can make serious problems for you in a court of law.

We should be **well-versed** in the legalities of self defense in our state not only for firearms, but for using *anything* (such as a bat) to defend ourselves, or even our hands. The moment you cause someone bodily harm, you will likely be forced to justify that use of force in a court. If you use excessive force when it was not seen as justified -- that is, if you escalated the seriousness of the situation -- YOU may be the one who ends up in jail.

When the police come and see your assailant bloodied and you, potentially unharmed, it may not look good. The law and the courts will decide if you were justified.

With pepper spray though, we're not physically putting a hand on the bad guy.

Here is an example of how I might handle a potential attacker. This is not legal advice:

If I feel as though a person who is approaching me has ill intent, I extend my arm and hand making a stop sign, forcefully telling them to "Stop right there!" I say it loudly and with conviction so others who may be around can hear. If they are undeterred, I say, "Stop or I'm going to pepper spray you!" If the person takes one more step toward me in a threatening way, I would likely let them have some pepper spray in the face.

A good-quality pepper spray will drop 95% of troublemakers immediately. Without physical interaction. They are not bloodied. They will experience discomfort for a while, but if I fear for my safety and told them to stop -- and they didn't -- well, that was their decision and we have a right to self defense. They will live. There is no permanent harm done and I have been a responsible citizen, having successfully mitigated legal liability on my part while de-escalating the threat.

Another interesting thing you can do with pepper spray is something termed "access denial".

Because pepper spray is an aerosol, sort of like a bug fogger or hairspray, let's say you have a living room near your front door and a long hallway or staircase leading to your sleeping quarters. If an intruder were breaking in from the front, you could deploy your spray down the stairs or hallway, then close your bedroom door, sequestering yourself inside to call the police (or ready yourself for further action) -- and no one will be coming down that hallway. Not unless you're dealing with a very industrious burglar who has a gas mask on hand, or perhaps one maddened by hard drug use. In all liklihood the pepper spray will make them leave the house.

Pepper sprays, gels, and foams can be **very** useful tools, but be sure to check your local laws regarding the possession and use of these defense items.

While i'm thinking about it, state laws and municipal codes in certain cities are getting pretty ridiculous these days, favoring the trespasser or criminal over the law abiding citizen and/or home-owner. You will know by the laws if you live in a state or city con-tolled by tyrants. If you can't possess a simple pepper spray where you live,

or if your state frowns upon you defending yourself and your loved ones in *any* way, I urge you to move. Make your home someplace where law abiding citizens' lives are valued more than that of the criminal element. This will ultimately behoove your preparedness plans. If local authorities look poorly on self de-fense, odds are they're going to be tyrannical in other ways as well. This does not bode well for us in an emergency setting. Private property rights comes to mind, but I digress. Just some food for thought.

I can recommend two brands of pepper spray:

"Sabre" and "Fox".

An off brand of pepper spray is like an off brand of bleach -- you'll never be sure what concentration level or quality you're getting, so just get the good stuff. You'll also want to replace these units every two or three years.

Price level for these items are anywhere from $12-18.

Pepper spray is an item I rarely leave home without. It can save you many problems and save the day, whether you are a firearms enthusiast or not.

He that gathereth in summer is a wise son: but he that sleepeth in harvest is a son that causeth shame.

Proverbs 10:5

Final Thoughts...

My friend, this concludes my introductory presentation on static home emergency preparedness. I hope it has helped and I'm truly happy you're interested.

Preparedness is a topic, a "hobby", that is *literally* without end. You'll never really be finished.

We are attempting to solve a set of problems.

We need to try and foresee what problems may occur in the future and try to solve them now, for the future.

Preparedness is problem solving.

What is a "problem" anyway? In preparedness terms, it's the loss of some THING that's necessary to sustain life. The loss of something (usually a system of some sort) which USED to be routine and predictable in daily life, but has been altered or otherwise LOST due to extraordinary or uncontrollable circumstances.

We usually get water from the tap. Now we can't -- that's a problem.

Society usually has law and order. Now it doesn't -- that's a problem.

As a preparedness-minded individual, you have to figure out how to solve problems. Ahead of time.

This is what we're doing in preparedness. Foreseeing problems and solving them before the problem actually occurs. If we wait to solve the problem, we might not be able to obtain the supplies or have the ability.

I say preparedness is never-ending because our solution(s) to problem(s) might break, run out, or otherwise stop working. The dynamics could change.

Life is fluid. An ever changing set of variables. All we can do is the best we can do. The key is that you MUST do SOMETHING. Choosing not to act is almost criminal.

The most important piece of equipment I can urge you to invest in is sitting on your shoulders, right between your ears. Invest in yourself. Invest in learning.

I hope this guide helps you on your way to being ready for an emergency situation. If YOU don't figure out a way to make ends meet for yourself, who will?

Keep learning, keep expanding your knowledge, keep thinking about preparedness, but whatever you do. . .

GET PREPARED.

They say the best time to plant a tree was seven years ago, but the next best time is today.

Apply this wisdom to your emergency preparedness.

You'll be glad you did.

May God bless you and keep you. May He let His light shine upon you and bring you peace.

If you need help, please reach out:

preblecowater@gmx.com